COMMUNAL WISDOM

Facilitators of communal discernment in parish life and religious congregations, spiritual directors and anyone drawn to depthing understandings and the practice of searching for God's will, both personally and communally, will be delighted and truly inspired with this concise, but comprehensive and instructive exposition of the experience of communal spirits in Christian decision making.

Expanding on the first edition of *Communal Wisdom*, descriptions of the ebb and flow of movements in the sifting and sorting of the spirits within individuals and groups is simply and clearly presented. The gleaning of valuable insights, including critical appraisal, from both secular and religious literature, brings a broadening and important validation of the author's approach. A special gem, central to this work, is the articulation of the contemplative way, generously supported by practical suggestions offered in the appendix.

This edition of *Communal Wisdom* is all the more helpful, formative and engendering of confidence because it reflects the learning of the author's lifetime of experience with his own journey, and those with whom he has journeyed individually and communally.

We live, and move, and find our being in mystery, as we come to know more of the God who 'walks' with us. *Communal Wisdom* reminds us that, as we journey with this mystery, we can draw from a rich tradition of discerning of spirits into which we are invited, and within which we are guided by so many signposts, that, if noticed, contemplated and followed, will indeed lead to the 'fullness of life' that Jesus so longed we would choose. *Communal Wisdom* provides an invaluable and most accessible tool for all involved in co-creating the church of the 21st Century.

Jill McCorquodale

Spiritual director and group facilitator, ministers throughout Australia and Asia, particularly with religious communities.

In *Communal Wisdom*, Brian Gallagher draws on his extensive experience in spiritual direction and working with groups in discernment to engage in conversation with classic and current writers on issues related to discernment in community. This concise volume is packed with practical insights into discernment processes that promote a contemplative and spiritual approach to decision making within communal contexts. These processes are summarised in Gallagher's '*Communal Wisdom* Approach' formulated to guide practitioners as they embark on the rich and rewarding journey of communal discernment in an increasingly complex world.

Peter S. Bentley

Rev. Dr Peter S. Bentley is Coordinator of Spiritual Formation, WellSpring Centre, Melbourne

Short and sweet might be a good description of this book on group discernment by Brian Gallagher. Fr Gallagher does a remarkably competent job of describing how he and his original co-author developed a way of helping groups to become more discerning in their interactions, more able to distinguish those reactions that come from God and lead to more honest and helpful discussions and decision making from those that not from God. He uses very helpful examples. And he does all this in less than forty pages. Amazing! I salute him and recommend this book to anyone who wants to help groups to work together in a more helpful way.

William A, Barry, sj

Fr William Barry, spiritual director, lecturer and co-author of The Practice of Spiritual Direction, is based at Boston College, Boston, USA.

SECOND EDITION REVISED & EXPANDED

COMMUNAL WISDOM

A WAY OF DISCERNMENT FOR
A PILGRIM CHURCH

BRIAN GALLAGHER MSC

COVENTRY
PRESS

Published in Australia by
Coventry Press
33 Scoresby Road
Bayswater Vic. 3153
Australia

ISBN 9780648360148

First edition published in 2009

This second, revised edition first published in 2018

Cataloguing-in-Publication entry is available from the National Library of Australia
http:/catalogue.nla.gov.au/.

Text design by Filmshot Graphics (FSG)
Cover design by Ian James - www.jgd.com.au

Printed in Australia

Contents

Foreword to the second edition

Much has happened in recent years that confirms the central importance of the insights of *Communal Wisdom*, and which more than justifies this new edition. Think, for example, of the leadership of Pope Francis, and the way he witnesses to the discernment of spirits at every point in his ministry and constantly invites the whole church into this practice. In his recent Apostolic Exhortation on holiness, Gaudete et Exsultate, Pope Francis writes at length about discernment. At one point, he says to all of us: "Always ask the Spirit what Jesus expects from you at every moment of your life and in every decision you must make, so as to discern its place in the mission you have received." (paragraph 23) In his Apostolic Exhortation on marriage and family, Amoris Laetitia, he puts conscience and the discernment of spirits at the centre of Christian moral life in the context of pastoral accompaniment within the ecclesial community.

Pope Francis has been a constant advocate for a more synodal church. Alongside the strong Catholic emphasis on the principle of unity or primacy in the church, expressed in the role of the bishop and the bishop of Rome, he points to the need for the principle of synodality. Synodality is a principle of participation. It involves the many, based on the theological conviction that the Spirit of God is given to every member of the church, and that listening to the Spirit means listening to all of God's people. Synodality finds expression in gatherings or councils of one kind or another at every level of church life, and these, if they are to function in a fully Christian way, will be moments of communal discernment. Synodal structures demand the practice of communal discernment.

The Catholic Church in Australia is undergoing an unparalleled crisis over the revelation of the history of sexual abuse of children by clergy, and the cover-up of this abuse by bishops. The pain of survivors has become public, and there is deep anger and a sense of being betrayed by church leaders. There is a wide-spread rejection of the culture of clericalism, and of the exclusion of women from leadership. There is a demand for far more lay leadership. In this situation, community discernment must have a fundamental role to play. The Australian bishops have initiated a process that will lead to a plenary council in 2020, in response both to the crisis we face, and to the plea of Pope Francis for a more synodal church. They have said that they seek the widest possible participation. The council itself, and the preparation and follow-up will obviously need to involve community discernment. We clearly are in great need of the revised *Communal Wisdom*.

Denis Edwards,
Professor of Theology
Australian Catholic University, Adelaide

Introduction

Much has been written about the principles and practices of individual, personal discernment. I review and affirm these principles in what follows and then apply them to communal discernment and decision making. The same principles and practices apply to communal discernment provided that the community, the group discerning, is functioning *as one*. This book is concerned with the communal experience of the spirits, God's Spirit and spirits not-of-God, and communal processes of making Christian decisions.

A basic given is that every person has a contribution to make and a right to speak:

> ... each of us has an inner divine light that gives us the guidance we need, but is often obscured by sundry forms of inner and outer interference.[1]

> The whole body of the faithful who have received an anointing that comes from the holy one (cf 1 John 2:20, 27) cannot be mistaken in belief... By this sense of faith, aroused and sustained by the Spirit of truth, the people of God, guided by the sacred magisterium which it faithfully obeys, receives not the word of human beings, but truly the word of God. (cf 1 Thessalonians 2:13)[2]

My experience of working with groups, however, has convinced me that a group is more than the summation of many individuals: the whole is greater than the sum of the parts. When group or communal discernment is sought, it seems critical to acknowledge that there is a *group* experience of God's

---

1   Parker Palmer, "The Clearness Committee: A Way of Discernment " *Weavings* 9, no. 4 (1988): 38. Palmer is cited in Wilkie Au and Noreen Cannon Au, *The Discerning Heart: Exploring the Christian Path* (New York: Paulist Press, 2006), 126.

2   Vatican II, "Lumen Gentium (Dogmatic Constitution on the Church)" in *The Documents of Vatican II*, #12.

Spirit and of spirits not-of-God, a *group* identity, and a *group* vulnerability, over and above the individual experiences of the members of the group. I believe that any group wishing to discern God's call to them *as a group* must first establish and reinforce their 'common base', their communal identity.

Discernment is primarily about *relationship*. In communal or group discernment, the concern is for the *group's* relationship with God, not merely the sum of all the individual relationships with God. Again, the whole is greater than the sum of the parts. And so, it becomes critical to look at the interplay of relationships within the group and the influence of these relationships on the way the group, as a whole, approaches God.

My experience facilitating group discernment has confirmed that quality time given to prayer and listening in the group, discovering the workings of God's Spirit and other spirits not-of-God *in the group*, is foundational in the discernment process. I discuss below some ways to build this foundation in the group, creating a discerning community, even before the introduction of any question or decision that needs to be discerned.

John English lists these facets of communal discernment:

- Community and communal experience are primary in living out our personal Christian life and discerning the 'will of God' in our personal lives
- Community is more than a collectivity of human beings
- Community is a lived reality, that is, more than a mental construct
- Communal discernment is not only a possibility; it is a necessity
- Communal spiritual consolation can be known and used in discernment.[3]

---

3   John J. English, "Communal Spiritual Consolation," *Review for Religious* 47, no. 6 (1988): 851.

In taking this approach, I distinguish between discernment of spirits and Christian decision making. Making good decisions in our lives – sometimes called discernment of God's Will – follows easily once we are familiar with the ways of God's Spirit and spirits not-of-God in our own experience. People who live a discerning way of life, attentive to the promptings of the Spirit of God and aware of how other spirits can pull them away from God, have no difficulty with decision making. So, too, with groups.

The approaches outlined here have been tested with groups of all sizes and from varying backgrounds. Always with another facilitator, I have worked with quite small groups and with groups of over one hundred members; we have worked with mixed parish groups, with religious communities, and with groups who had little history of working together. We ask only these pre-requisites: that all be willing to give time to prayerful listening, and that, to the best of their awareness, all come freely and open to God's Word.

Initially, I discuss the ways of the spirits – in individual lives, then in groups. Ignatius Loyola first noted that the spirits work differently for people at different stages of their spiritual development. For example, there is marked contrast in how the spirits attract a person whose basic disposition is towards God and a person whose basic orientation is away from God. Most people are in the former category: they are people who are sincerely committed to God's ways, but still, at times, find themselves behaving in an opposite way. 'I don't always do what I want to do' wrote Paul (Romans 7:15). In what follows, I focus on these people and groups.

This edition of *Communal Wisdom* is a revised and expanded development of the first edition, co-authored with Sue Richardson.[4]

---

4   Sue Richardson and Brian Gallagher, *Communal Wisdom* (Box Hill, Vic: Heart of Life, 2009).

Chapter 1

The Ways of the Spirits

Discernment rests on the habit of our recognising in our inner life the signs of God's Spirit inviting to life and the signs of spirits not-of-God inviting to non-life. The workings of the spirits in us are quite consistent, even while quite subtle. Once we have named for ourselves the signs of how the 'good and bad' spirits work in us, we are well placed to recognise the recurring attractions of the spirits in our lives. There are 'rules for discernment', but I believe that the rules are most helpful when discovered personally, integrated in one's experience of the spirits.

The traditional terminology of 'spirits' refers to one's inner needs and desires, spontaneous impulses and affective habits, thoughts, imaginings, emotions, attractions and repulsions in one's experience of life. Discernment is the process of sifting these inner movements, naming them and understanding where they come from and where they lead. The spirits are defined, in fact, by the direction in which a movement leads, not by the felt content of the movement. In what follows, I develop this approach from the experience of the spirits.

God's Spirit

To begin with God's Spirit: in our teaching and facilitation, the writing of Herbert Alphonso is most instructive.[5] Alphonso's focus on one's 'personal vocation' as an expression of one's experience of God's call gives a framework in which to study the very personal, individual ways in which God's Spirit works. We

---

5   Herbert Alphonso, *The Personal Vocation* (Rome: Centrum Ignatianum Spiritualitatis, 1990).

guide people to reflect on the graced moments of their lives, the experiences of gift, the images of their lives that energise and call them to life, and the times of decision making that have proven unquestionably life-giving. Reflecting on personal experience in these ways helps people to notice not only the fruits of God's Spirit working – the peace, joy, harmony that Paul describes – but also the inner signs when the Spirit is active and inviting – maybe the inner 'tingle' or excitement, the unquestionable 'knowing', the new level of energy, or the call to life.

For example, Ignatius Loyola recorded that he found himself 'cheerful and satisfied' when God's Spirit had touched him. Teresa of Avila noticed 'all the things of God made me happy.' These are attempts to describe the felt consolation from the Spirit of God – the 'love, joy, peace, patience...' named by Paul (Galatians 5:22). In discernment terminology, *consolation* is a rather technical word to describe an inner movement towards God, towards life – a movement, in fact, that is not always 'consoling' in the everyday usage of that word. Examples of consolation, in themselves, do not define consolation. What defines experiences of consolation is that they are always movements towards God, always life-giving.

'Desolation' is the opposite experience, the fruit of following some spirit not-of-God. From experience, I develop below that experiences of desolation are not always 'desolate' in the usual understanding of the word.

People use different words to describe the fruits of the Spirit in their experience. Indeed, this is to be encouraged: using personal language in speaking of one's experience helps to claim the experience for oneself. For example:

> Experiences of inner joy and peace, moods of confidence and encouragement to faith, a sense of being in harmony with oneself and with God, times

of true creativity, and so on, are true consolation, signs of the presence of the Spirit...[6]

There is a sense of our own worth... something lifts from us, we feel lighter, liberated... we grow in compassion and sensitivity to the needs of others.[7]

For committed people, the experience of consolation is always on an affective level. Later in the chapter, I note that spirits not-of God also produce affective responses in people whose basic orientation is towards God. And so, discernment of the Spirit of God for these committed people whose orientation is towards God, is a discernment of one's feelings. One's feelings do point to whichever spirit is at work, but they need to be discerned.

Most often, people seem to recognise the fruits of the Spirit before they realise that they have, in fact, responded to the invitation of God's Spirit. Spiritual directors are well prepared to help people name these fruits, to deepen their awareness and appreciation of the felt 'good' or the 'peace' – or, sometimes, the rather disturbing sense of being invited to some new truth in themselves – all experiences of deepening faith and love. These are experiences of consolation.

This movement towards God, towards life, will show itself invariably in the way the fruits of the Spirit overflow into people's relationships. When people are true to the invitation of God's Spirit in their lives, their relationships flourish: people become more open to others, more accepting, more tolerant of others. For God's gifts are given to individuals personally, but not privately: the gifts are given personally, but for the sake of others. Paul added that God's gifts are given for the edification of the whole community (Ephesians 4:12). In other words, the Spirit of God is always constructive: it deepens relationships, builds community, brings communion.

---

6   David Lonsdale, *Dance to the Music of the Spirit* (London: Darton, Longman & Todd, 1992), 62.

7   Patrick O'Sullivan, *Prayer and Relationships* (Melbourne, Vic: David Lovell Publications, 2008), 111-2.

Once the fruits have been recognised, we encourage people to look back to name how and when God's invitation or God's gift was offered to them. It seems that many people hear and follow the promptings of God's Spirit in such an instinctive way that they notice the fruits of the Spirit without having named precisely the initial signs of God's invitation, the signs that they were responding to in themselves. Knowing that God's Spirit is quite consistent and faithful, it seems important to articulate these signs, not only for the sake of learning, but also so that the same signs will be recognised in the future, even in more subtle situations.

These 'signs' are quite personal: for one, it might be the invitation to take a risk; for another, an unexpected sense of new energy; for yet another, an 'at-homeness' that the person has learned to trust. All are signs of life – and lead to life.

Spirits not-of-God

Sometimes, unwittingly, we are deceived by other spirits, spirits which are not-of-God and which lead us away from life, more into confusion, isolation from others and lack of love. These are experiences of *desolation*, a technical term to describe a movement away from God. This movement away from God can happen despite ourselves: it is not a question of morality or a choice to sin. And, as mentioned, it does not always feel desolate.

Spirits not-of-God work against God's Spirit. The direction in which the spirits not-of-God attract is the very opposite of the direction in which God's Spirit is leading. Spirits not-of-God work to hold one back from God, to resist God's invitation, to break any true relationship with God. Discernment is always about relationship with God.

I have learned from experience that spirits not-of-God attack where they are most likely to have success: at a person's point of vulnerability. Ignatius Loyola favoured the image of a 'shrewd army commander' who studied the place he wished to conquer to find where the defences were weakest.[8] This invariably happens via false messages that we give ourselves, what Ignatius called 'fallacious reasoning'[9]. Though the messages are quite false, they are heard as true, because they appeal to our vulnerability and sound credible. This insight, confirmed by experience, has helped many people to understand how unwittingly they have taken a direction in life that has not been life-giving, or made some important decision that has gone wrong.

Every person has some vulnerability: vulnerability has been called humanity's common patrimony.[10] Luigi Rulla speaks of unconscious inconsistencies in human nature: he found in his research into Christian vocation that 'psychodynamic factors may influence the degree of freedom with which the individual is disposed to the action of grace.'[11] When speaking of the human experience of freedom, Rulla speaks of one's 'essential freedom', God's gift of inner freedom, and one's 'effective freedom', one's experience of *unfreedom*.[12] Rulla applied his argument to discernment of spirits:

> When a person responds because the object is consciously or unconsciously perceived as something which also favours his own self-esteem, this does not necessarily favour self-transcendence and the internalisation of the ideal... For example, one may be attracted to and aspire to an imitation

---

8   Ignatius Loyola, *The Spiritual Exercises of St. Ignatius Loyola*, ed. George E. Gans (Chicago, IL: Loyola University Press, 1998), #327.

9   *Ibid.*, #329.

10   Luigi M. Rulla, *Anthropology of the Christian Vocation* (Rome: Gregorian University Press, 1986), 14.

11   Luigi M. Rulla, "The Discernment of Spirits and Christian Anthropology," *Gregorianum* 59, no. 3 (1978): 541.

12   Bernard J. Lonergan, *Insight: A Study of Human Understanding* (London: Longmans, Green and Co., 1957), 619-24, 92-3. I use the term *unfreedom* to describe the human experience of limited or lack of inner freedom.

of the generosity of Christ, while in reality and in
the last analysis, one gives in order to receive.[13]

This is an example of what Rulla calls a choice for an
apparent good, flowing out of a place of *unfreedom,* a place
of vulnerability. Rulla understands such *unfreedom* as a
person's inner needs or attachments, usually unconscious, but
affecting one's behaviour.

One's vulnerable spot has its own history in one's early
life experience, but it is not of one's own making or choice.[14]
Psychiatrist Karen Horney explains how one becomes
vulnerable. She wrote of 'the tyranny of the *should'*, suggesting
that the *'shoulds'* which most people seem to ingest in early
years leave them vulnerable in later years. Horney gives
numerous examples of how vulnerability develops:

> (The neurotic) sets to work to mould himself into a
> supreme being of his own making. He holds before
> his soul his image of perfection and unconsciously
> tells himself 'this is how you *should* be – and to be
> this idealized self is all that matters. You should be
> able to endure everything, to understand everything,
> to like everybody, to be always productive... to be
> the utmost of honesty, generosity, considerateness,
> justice, dignity, courage, unselfishness...'[15]

Horney's reference to 'the neurotic' is her way of naming
what she sees as universal human experience: all people develop
some vulnerability in this way.

Our vulnerable spots are quite personal, too: examples
might be a need for affirmation, a sensitivity to criticism, a
fear of what others think of me, a rigidity in relationships, a
tendency to de-value oneself. We notice that more often than

---

13   Rulla, "The Discernment of Spirits and Christian Anthropology," 545.

14   Brian Gallagher, *Taking God to Heart* (Strathfield, NSW: St Pauls, 2008), 35-40.

15   Karen Horney, *Neurosis and Human Growth* (New York: W W Norton & Co,
     1950), 64-5.

not, our vulnerability connects with our self-esteem, with how we see ourselves. And in some sense, this vulnerable spot or 'weak spot' in our make-up will always be with us. And because this point of vulnerability is ever-present, people gradually notice a predictability about the way spirits not-of-God tempt with their false messages. The patterns in the ways we are tempted and the patterns in our behaviour will often give us the first clue to our vulnerability.

Awareness of the inner dictates described by Horney can enable behavioural change, but the point of vulnerability remains, as illustrated in Paul's experience when he prayed to God to take away 'the thorn in his flesh.' But no, it remains as the constant reminder that 'my grace is sufficient for you.' (2 Corinthians 12:7-9) One's vulnerable spot offers the same ever-present reminder that one cannot save oneself, that one is utterly dependant on God's grace.

Even in the experience of spirits that are not-of-God, people seem to notice the fruits of the spirit first. It can happen, for example, that sincere decisions later turn sour – the 'fruits' turn out to be more destructive than life-giving. When people notice this, we encourage them to look back to the time of the decision making and name the voice they were listening to in themselves when they made the decision. Naming that initial message will bring awareness also of the appeal the message was making. At least in retrospect, it's possible to recognise the point of vulnerability and why the message seemed true at the time.

This is not to be self-critical or self-blaming: indeed, it seems important to acknowledge that the initial decision was made in all sincerity.

Only now, in retrospect, it is possible to say that what seemed true at the time, in fact, is false. Clear thinking is needed here: because the temptation came via 'fallacious reasoning', only clear true reasoning will counter the work of these spirits not-of-God. Once a person recognises this dynamic, they are able to say with conviction 'I do not, in fact, believe that message'.

The contemplative way

I strongly encourage a contemplative approach to reflection on one's experience. This approach is integral to my ministry of spiritual direction and discernment. Contemplative listening makes possible a deeper, truer noticing of the ways of the spirits in experience. It has been called 'seeing with the eyes of God'.[16]

John of the Cross wrote that 'contemplation is to receive'.[17] This has prompted many to see Mary, the Mother of Jesus, as the prototype of the contemplative person. Mary received the Word of God literally in her womb and symbolically in every facet of her being. As I wrote in *Taking God to Heart*, 'the womb is symbol of complete openness and receptivity, of expectant waiting, of total surrender, and, finally, of giving flesh and birth to God's Word. The womb is pure receptivity, waiting to receive what will begin the life-process within it.'[18] Such openness and receptivity to what is given is inherent to the contemplative way.

Human people are by nature contemplative beings. In many cultures, however, the human tendency towards independence and self-sufficiency can be a strong obstacle to 'receiving' for many people. The contemplative nature yearns to know what is real, what is true, and what is good – ultimately what is of God – in one's experience. Because discernment is concerned with what is of God, I argue that a contemplative approach is basic to the practice of discernment and to the process of becoming discerning.

---

16   See Gallagher, *Taking God to Heart*, 33. quoting Abraham J. Heschel, *The Prophets* (New York: Harper & Row, 1962), 138, 212.

17   John of the Cross, "The Living Flame of Love," in *The Collected Works of St. John of the Cross*, ed. Kieran Kavanaugh and Otilio Rodriguez (Washington DC: Institute of Carmelite Studies, 1973), stanza 3.36.

18   Gallagher, *Taking God to Heart*, 28.

This approach asks for an intentional focus outside of oneself. Whether the object of contemplation is a beautiful flower or another person or the Word of God in prayer, the focus is entirely on the other, with no expectations or pre-conceived ideas about whatever the other will reveal of itself. It asks 'a simple, open presence to what is.'[19] Walter Burghardt defined contemplation as 'a long loving look at the real':

> The real I look at, I do not analyse it or argue it. I do not describe or define it. I am one with it... I enter into it... To contemplate is to be in love.[20]

In his practical suggestions to help a person cultivate a contemplative attitude, Burghardt encourages a sense of play and festivity. Most of all, he says, 'don't try to possess the object of your delight... and don't expect to profit from contemplation.'[21]

Barry speaks of the same contemplative attitude as an experience of 'transcendence':

> Contemplation leads to, or rather is, an experience of transcendence, of self-forgetfulness of everyone and everything else except the contemplated object... let the other be himself or herself or itself... be open to surprise or newness...[22]

Both contemplation and discernment mean openness to surprise and newness – an attitude of interior freedom, often called 'holy indifference',[23] a basic pre-requisite in discernment. Remaining indifferent means staying open to God's Spirit.

---

19 Tilden Edwards, *Spiritual Director, Spiritual Companion: Guide to Tending the Soul* (New York: Paulist, 2001), 4.

20 Walter Burghardt, "Contemplation: A Long Loving Look at the Real" (paper presented at the National Federation of Spiritual Directors, Camarillo, CA 1975), 8-10.

21 *Ibid.*

22 William A. Barry, "The Contemplative Attitude in Spiritual Direction," *Review for Religious* 35, no. 6 (1976): 821.

23 See, for example, John J. English, *Spiritual Freedom* (Guelph, Ontario: Loyola House, 1973), 46-50. English discusses Ignatius Loyola's use of the term 'indifference' in his *Spiritual Exercises.*

Francis de Sales explains indifference: 'If I like only pure water, what does it matter to me whether it is served in a goblet of gold or in one of glass, since in either case I drink only the water.'[24]

The essential attitude of waiting on God's Revelation is well described by John Chapman, Benedictine Abbot. When one approaches prayer in this contemplative way, Chapman emphasises waiting on God, wanting God, but having to wait on God's gift:

> The time of prayer is spent in the act of waiting on God. It is an idiotic state and feels like the completest waste of time... The strangest phenomenon is we begin to wonder whether we mean anything at all, and if we are addressing anyone... even the word 'God' seems to mean nothing. If we feel this curious and paradoxical condition, we are on the right road.[25]

Chapman was strongly influenced by John of the Cross. When talking of waiting on God, when nothing else is being asked, John says:

> ... allow the soul to remain in rest and quietude... [We] must be content simply with a loving and peaceful attentiveness to God, and live without the concern, without the effort, and without the desire to taste or feel God.[26]

John's 'attentiveness to God' is Chapman's 'waiting on God' even when nothing seems to be happening in one's prayer. One may experience strong desire for God, which John of the Cross distinguishes from 'desire to feel God's presence'. For many, the temptation is to relieve the apparent emptiness of the prayer by

---

24 Francis de Sales, *Treatise on the Love of God* (Rochford, IL: Tan Books, 1963), Book 9, chapter 4.

25 John Chapman, *Spiritual Letters* (London: Sheed & Ward, 1983), Appendix.

26 John of the Cross, "Dark Night," in *The Collected Works of St. John of the Cross*, I,10.4.

looking elsewhere, to some other way of prayer or some inspiring book, rather than waiting on God. God is experienced in the waiting, though God's presence is not felt. I believe that this is true of a contemplative attitude to all of life's endeavours.[27]

The *Awareness Examen* prayer, itself a contemplative prayer, is a recommended way to grow in awareness of the movements of the spirits in one's experience.[28] In its basic form, the prayer suggests that we quieten ourselves, maybe at the end of the day, we thank God for the gifts of the day, and we simply ask God to bring into our awareness whatever of the day God wants us to re-live now.

And then we wait on God's revelation, on whatever God chooses to bring into our awareness – some memory of the day, a meeting, a word that touched us, a mood that seems to have stayed with us. We may need to re-live a memory of some experience that we didn't fully appreciate at the time, or we may need to sit quietly with whatever has come back to us, asking God about its message for us now. Essentially, we wait on God's Word. And quite spontaneously, we respond to what we hear – maybe in gratitude, maybe an apology for past mistakes, or maybe a prayer for more clarity or understanding of God's Word to us.

I have noticed time and again that the fruit of this prayer, prayed regularly, is that people become more sensitive to the ways of God in their everyday lives, more attentive to the signs of God's presence and invitation to them. I encourage such prayer for people wishing to be more discerning in their lives and for groups committed to communal discernment.

---

27 William Barry writes of a 'contemplative attitude to life' in "Spiritual Direction: the Empirical Approach," *America* 24 April 1976.

28 George Aschenbrenner, "Consciousness Examen," *Review for Religious* 31, no. 1 (1972): 14-21. A simplified adaptation of the prayer is found in Brian Gallagher, *Pray as You Are* (Sydney, NSW: Nelen Yubu, 1999), 24.

Chapter 2

The Ways of the Spirits in group experience

A group's contemplative listening flows through the interplay of the prayer of the individuals in the group and the group's sharing of their prayer with one another. Facilitators, also listening contemplatively, notice the signs of the spirits working in the group's prayer.

In the ministry of individual spiritual direction, we've found it imperative that the spiritual director notice movements in themself at the same time as listening to the person who comes for spiritual direction. These inner movements in the listening director will often be the first clue to recognising the spirit in the experience being shared. So, too, in a facilitator's listening to a group's sharing: the inner movements that the facilitator notices in themself, properly interpreted by the facilitator from past experience, give the clue to recognising the spirit operating in the group.[29]

The facilitator will often need to ask, 'What's happening in the group at the moment?' 'What is the present mood of the group telling us?' 'What spirit are we listening to right now?' It's as though the facilitator listens on behalf of the group – and invites the group to come to the same awareness.

Facilitators clearly need to know *about* discernment; more importantly, they need to *be* discerning people themselves.

---

29 This approach in *Communal Wisdom* is recommended also by Lon Fendall, Jan Wood, and Bruce Bishop, *Practising Discernment Together: Finding God's Way Forward in Decision Making.* (Newberg, OR: Barclay Press, 2007). Bishop encourages directors/facilitators to develop their personal 'discernment portfolio'.

God's Spirit in a group

We encourage the members of a group to pray in a contemplative way, and to share with others around how God has gifted them *as a group*. As with personal discernment, this process deepens awareness of both the fruits of God's Spirit working in the group and the signs to look for in themselves when the Spirit of God is inviting the group to new life. Or the group may pray over past growth times for them *as a group,* or past decisions that the group has made that have been fruitful for them *as a group.*

Just as noted when describing personal discernment, it seems to be common experience with groups also that the fruits of the spirit – the evidence of new life in the group -- are noticed first. When this happens, we invite the group to look back at how they actually made their group decisions or how they knew God's gift to them at that earlier time. We invite the group to name in retrospect the signs that were present at the earlier time, signs that are often quite subtle and easily overlooked. These are the signs that God's Spirit is inviting the group to new life. They are unique to each group and are likely to recur often in the group's experience. Examples might be a group's sense that it is being called to live with more trust in Providence, or a group's awareness that its best decisions have been when the group has been inclusive of others, or a group's experience of acting freely, without self-interest.

Again, it seems important to note that these signs or invitations of God's Spirit are not always cosy and comfortable: in times when the group has unwittingly taken a wrong direction, the invitations of God's Spirit will be challenging, even disturbing and unsettling. For some groups, to hear and follow these invitations of the Spirit can be quite painful.

But still, they *are* the signs of God's Spirit inviting a group to new life. The *fruits* that come from the group's honest response to the invitation – or the *consolation* that the group experiences – confirm for the group that it has, in fact, followed the good Spirit.

And again, as seen in examples of individual discernment, such communal consolation will surely show itself in relationships, relationships within the group and relationships beyond the group. The group's ministry will bear even greater fruit.

Spirits not-of-God in a group

But groups, too, have vulnerable spots – and most groups need time to become aware of their vulnerability. Because some in the group need more time than others, then the group needs time. And because some in the group will not immediately identify with the revealed vulnerable spot, again the group as a whole needs time to own its vulnerability. To be clear: a group's vulnerable spot is not necessarily the vulnerable spot of every individual in the group, or even of any one individual in the group. This is quite a different experience for a group.

For example, many groups suffer from a false humility, often under the guise of virtue: 'It's better that people think poorly of us...' 'We don't have the presence of other groups...' 'We've always seen ourselves as behind the scenes...' Or some groups are quite unfree, fixated on a need for security or a need to be well thought-of: 'We can't afford such risks...' 'Our group doesn't have the resources...' 'We're fearful...'

In our facilitation, we have met groups which innocently put conditions on God's response to them: 'If we had done such-and-such differently, God would have provided.' Though members of the group may not realise that such statements / assumptions amongst themselves betray deep vulnerability – even quite an unhealthy group self-image – often people do begin to notice unloving behaviour in their group. We have noticed groups unwittingly manipulating others, judging others in prejudicial ways, isolating themselves from others, even relating harshly and unfeelingly amongst themselves. Such behaviour is the result of having followed some spirit not-of-God, and more often than not, without having adverted to this habit.

In a perfect parallel with the way spirits not-of-God seem to tempt in personal discernment, groups then need to look back to discover the false messages they had listened to at their point of vulnerability. In other words, groups, too, are tempted away from life, away from God. Our vulnerabilities, our weak spots, are ripe ground for spirits not-of-God, appealing to the group's vulnerability. In the examples above, such spirits will affirm a group's poor self-image, or will make a group's fear of risk sound plausible. Then the group will be left feeling safe and secure, even pleased with itself, but it would be a pseudo-security, and quite false -- indeed, a place of *desolation*. Such falsity needs to be exposed.

Reflection on past group experiences of decision making can be helpful for this purpose. Many groups are able to quote major decisions that they have made according to their best lights, but that have turned out poorly, indeed decisions which later they have wanted to reverse. What they thought was the right decision at the time proved to be a poor decision. We encourage the group then to re-live the time of making their decision and name the voice they were listening to – and believing – at the time. From the vantage point of their new awareness, many groups see quickly enough why the voice they were listening to seemed credible in the past. Now, because the group is in touch with its vulnerability, people are able to reject the false voice and recommit to the true call of God.

Equally important in the process is for the group to look back and discover the quieter, more gentle voice of God's Spirit, which was also present in their experience, but was overlooked at the time. Again paralleling individual discernment, common experience for groups seems to be that the voices of the counter spirits, the spirits not-of-God, tend to be louder, more demanding and in some sense more inviting, because of the group's vulnerability. But God's Spirit is always present, always offering new life, even though not always heard. Again, naming such presence, even in retrospect, means that the group will be more sensitive to hearing God's Spirit in the future.

In summary, these are the frequently encountered signs of the spirits in group discernment:

	Paul : Galatians	Gallagher
Good Spirit	love joy peace generosity community	freedom reconciliation community energy for mission
Other spirits	quarrels dissensions isolation unfreedom	disagreements factions unfree decisions

Chapter 3

Approaches to Communal Discernment

Literature on communal discernment or group decision making comes from both secular and religious writing. A secular example is Harrison Owen, who does not talk of discernment as such, but uses spirit language when describing 'how organisations transform'. When referring to the spirit within a group, he insists that 'Spirit is the most important thing.'[30] In the presence of the Spirit, 'there is excitement, innovation, and what we might call *inspired* (in-spirit) performance.' Owen has facilitated quite large groups, employing what is called *Open Space technology*. He uses the term 'spirit' in the sense of 'team spirit', 'high spirits', even 'the eternal Spirit, the mother of us all'. Owen refers to the experience of what he calls 'pure Spirit' which a group glimpses when inspired.[31]

Communal experience

When facilitating groups, Owen says the goal is to allow the spirit of the group, the group's own inner power to emerge. The fruits of such an emergence are 'high learning', 'high play', true community, and increased efficiency[32] – in striking parallel to my understanding of the fruits of God's Spirit, discussed above. As well, Owen introduces the term 'soul pollution' in organisations – characterised by burnout, stress, absenteeism, employee turnover, and various forms of addiction – to speak of contrary experiences in a group, blocking any awareness

30 Harrison Owen, *The Power of Spirit* (San Francisco, CA: Berrett-Koehler Publishing Inc, 2000), 2, 7.

31 *Ibid.*, 104.

32 *Ibid.*, 118-25.

of group spirit.[33] This terminology also has a clear parallel with my understanding of the ways of spirits not-of-God. Owen's appreciation of the *communal* experience of the spirits permeates his work.

Elizabeth Liebert uses the term 'social discernment'. Liebert brings a contemplative, prayerful approach to social analysis and systems theory, emphasising the value of seeing the discerning group 'as a whole person (that is, a system).'[34]

In support of the development of a communal focus, Brian O'Leary stresses 'corporate identity',[35] Elizabeth Liebert speaks of a discerning group 'as a whole person',[36] and John Futrell argues that the first, *sine qua non* condition for communal discernment is the consciousness of 'a profound common vision... a profound common identity, a profound communion.'[37] Sue Richardson and I use the term 'our common base'.[38]

Mary Benet McKinney develops a 'shared wisdom' approach to group decision making.[39] McKinney begins with the theology of collegiality from Vatican Council II. Though she insists on the communion of a group, and that God's Spirit is active in all people, McKinney seems unaware of the communal experience of the Spirit and of any spirits not-of-God, as distinct from the many separate individual experiences of the spirits. In the final analysis, McKinney equates God's Spirit with the majority opinion. I disagree with this approach: I do not believe that majority opinion is necessarily a sign of the Spirit of God.

33 *Ibid.*, 114.

34 Elizabeth Liebert, *The Soul of Discernment* (Louisville, Ky: Westminster John Knox Press, 2015), 41.

35 Brian O'Leary, "Communal Discernment: An Ignatian Perspective," *Religious Life Review* 43, no. 1 (2004): 20-4.

36 Elizabeth Liebert, *The Soul of Discernment*, 41.

37 John Carroll Futrell, "Ignatian Discernment," *Studies in the Spirituality of the Jesuits* II, no. 2 (1970), 70.

38 Sue Richardson and Brian Gallagher, *Communal Wisdom*, 19.

39 Mary Benet McKinney, *Sharing Wisdom: A Process for Group Decision Making* (Allen, Texas: Tabor Publishing, 1987), 43, 51.

George Schemel and Judith Roemer see consensus in a group as the goal of communal discernment,[40] equating the Spirit of God with consensus. They, too, overlook the communal experience of the spirits. The *Communal Wisdom* approach, outlined below, argues rather that God's Spirit in a group may be quite a different experience from the experience of any one member of the group, from any experience reached by a vote of members, and from the result of any apparent consensus in a group.

Donna Markham develops what she has named *Spiritlinking* leadership to work through resistance to change which leaders meet in groups.[41]   Though Markham uses quite different terminology, her work acknowledges a group experience of resistance and of the possibility of growth to fruitful community and mission. Markham's insistence that community building is the desired outcome of her process parallels my understanding of the fruits of God's Spirit at work and her recognition of the 'subtle resistances' parallels my understanding of the work of spirits not-of-God.

First Jesuit experience of discernment

Several writers, for example Jules Toner[42] and John Futrell[43] base their discussion of communal discernment on the experience of the first Jesuit Fathers, discerning their future in 1538, in what was called 'the deliberation'. Toner defines 'communal discernment of God's Will' as 'a process undertaken by a community as a community for the purpose of judging

40   George Schemel and Judith Roemer, "Communal Discernment," *Review for Religious* 40, no. 6 (1981): 832.

41   Donna J. Markham, *Spiritlinking Leadership: Working with Resistance to Organisational Change* (New York: Paulist Press, 1999).

42   Jules J. Toner, "A Method for Communal Discernment of God's Will," *Studies in the Spirituality of Jesuits* III, no. 4 (1971).

43   John Carroll Futrell, "Communal Discernment," *Studies in the Spirituality of Jesuits* IV, no. 5 (1972).

what God is calling that community to do.'[44] Similarly, Futrell speaks of a group's coming to recognise the Word of God 'to the whole community',[45] once individual members have noticed 'the difference between the Word of God to an individual and to the whole community.'[46] This often asks that some individuals are invited to change their original position. Futrell noticed also that groups which had used this method develop a growing sense of bondedness with one another, of 'real interior communion,' supporting my own experience.

In order to enhance this common vision and spirituality, communal discernment asks that all members of the group be open to God's Spirit in their own minds and hearts *and in one another*. Pre-requisite to communal discernment is personal prayer, mutual respect and love, openness to one another and trust in one another's good will.

Lonsdale, too, bases his reflection on the experience of the first Jesuit Fathers.[47] His basic pre-requisites are helpful: the importance of prayer, the deepening of a group's trust in one another, and the need to agree on 'ground rules'. Lonsdale comments that one individual in a group who is in a place of desolation, for example, can easily influence others in the group, but he does not seem to have an appreciation of group identity.

Quaker discernment

The practice of discernment is integral to the Quaker way, and an excellent example of communal discernment. Jo Farrow, a Quaker herself for many years, claims:

---

44   Jules J. Toner, "A Method for Communal Discernment of God's Will," *Studies in the Spirituality of Jesuits* III, no. 4 (1971): 124.

45   John Carroll Futrell, "Ignatian Discernment," *Studies in the Spirituality of Jesuits* II, no. 2 (1970): 70.

46   John Carroll Futrell, "Communal Discernment," *Studies in the Spirituality of Jesuits* IV, no. 5 (1972): 179.

47   David Lonsdale, *Dance to the Music of the Spirit,* 104-9.

There is a sense in which discernment *is* the Quaker tradition, in a communal as well as an individual context... There is no doubt that early Friends saw themselves as living in a new age of the Spirit.[48]

In meetings, the Quaker approach is called the 'Clearness Process'. Alan Kolp lists the six characteristics of this process, which he says are all simultaneously in play: trust and patience, belief 'that God has a desire for us' and that God's desire is 'knowable', being open, paying attention in a responsible way, remaining hopeful, and that the process is communal.[49]

Farrow names similar aspects of the Quaker approach to discernment, in both prayer meetings and business meetings, emphasising the discipline of waiting, the 'test of unity', and (she says, 'perhaps less wholesome') the 'test of the cross':

'Waiting' is one of the key words in the Quaker understanding of discernment and, linked with patience, it constituted one of the major tests of whether an individual leading represented a genuine prompting of the Spirit...

It may mean that a very long process of waiting and listening is involved that is irksome to those who believe they can see very clearly how things should proceed. But the 'test of unity' is another of the ways in which Friends have judged whether there has been a true discerning of the will of God.[50]

Lon Fendall, Jan Wood and Bruce Bishop, also writing in the Quaker tradition, emphasise the same process of listening and waiting in silence and the same desire for group unity.[51] These

---

48 Jo Farrow, "Discernment in the Quaker Tradition," *The Way Supplement* 64, no. Spring (1989): 51.

49 Alan Kolp, "The Clearness Process: A Way Opens," *The Way* 47, no. 1&2 (2008): 177-8.

50 Farrow, "Discernment in the Quaker Tradition," 57-8.

51 Fendall, Wood, and Bishop, *Practising Discernment Together*, 99, 103-10.

two elements of the approach, the need to wait patiently and the test of unity, are in common with most other approaches to discernment. Waiting on God is of the essence of contemplative prayer, as emphasised earlier. Moreover, God's Spirit always builds community, 'the test of unity'. In communal discernment, this is evident initially in the unity of the group, the fruit of God's Spirit.

As mentioned above, group unity does not mean that all members of the group necessarily have the same opinion, as in consensus. Rather, all agree to abide by the group decision, as agreed upon in the 'ground rule'. Michael Sheeran makes the important observation that the Quaker process 'builds on the insight that God's invitations are more likely to be found in the positive unity of a group than in majority votes.'[52] As well, this process of discernment

> rejects the creation of 'us' and 'them'... rejects the demonising of those with whom we disagree or those we find ourselves fearing... and transcends the need to play politics or persuade others of our view...'[53]

Ideally, this is the unity to be sought in any approach to communal discernment.

Lonsdale stresses the 'contemplative silence' of Quaker meetings and draws out the many similarities he sees between an Ignatian and a Quaker approach to discernment.[54] One similarity, he observes, is that both traditions clearly recognise that God has already planted wisdom in each individual and group.[55]

---

52 Michael J. Sheeran, "Ignatius and the Quakers," *The Way Supplement* 68, no. Summer (1990): 91.

53 Fendall, Wood, and Bishop, *Practising Discernment Together*, 127-8.

54 Lonsdale, *Dance to the Music of the Spirit*, 143.

55 Katherine Marie Dyckman, Mary Garvin and Elizabeth Liebert, *Spiritual Exercises Reclaimed:Uncovering Liberating Possibilities for Women* (New York: Paulist, 2001), 301.

Granted that, Farrow makes an essential observation of a major difference:

> In spite of its stress on inwardness, discernment in the Quaker tradition has not been about subjective states of mind and very little attention has been given to feelings of consolation and desolation. Unlike Ignatian spirituality which explores both states and draws inferences from them, Quaker spirituality has been very little concerned with the affective life. It is both its strength and its weakness that it has been more preoccupied with the ethical demands of the inward light and has not chosen to concern itself with the emotional life.[56]

Farrow's comment that Quaker spirituality and discernment give little attention to individuals' affective life, seeing this as both a strength and a weakness in their approach, is significant. The Quaker approach does seem to overlook any direct focus on group consolation and desolation and on personal and group freedom. At the same time, it would appear that, even without the terminology, the Friends presume on the need for such inner freedom. It may well be the value of the practice of prolonged silent prayer, integral to the Quaker approach. Silent contemplative prayer bears fruit in deepening inner freedom, personal and communal, even without awareness that this is happening. This prayer is the strength of Quaker discernment.

---

56 Farrow, "Discernment in the Quaker Tradition," 59.

Chapter 4

The Communal Wisdom approach

In what follows, I review learnings from the approaches outlined and an approach that Sue Richardson and I have developed, called *Communal Wisdom*.[57] With Futrell and Owen, the *Communal Wisdom* approach emphasises the *communal* experience of God's Spirit and spirits not-of-God. The discerning group, *as group*, as well as every individual in the group, is encouraged to claim its voice. My initial conviction that a group is more than the sum of many individuals permeates this approach to communal discernment.

I stress that the communal experience of the spirits is quite a different experience from the sum of the personal experiences of the members of the group. The communal experience of prayer, of consolation and desolation, requires a marked shift in thinking and praying for most groups.

I discuss initially how a group prepares itself for discernment. Most groups need careful facilitation to aid listening to the Word of God to the whole community. Normally, a group will discuss the 'ground rules' at the beginning of their process, including how the final communal decision will be made. Usually ground rules do not necessarily ask for consensus amongst the members of the group. It may well be that the group senses the Spirit's invitation to them, as a group, through the contribution of only one member's prayer. In other words, when the group hears the communal invitation of the Spirit of God, even individuals who may have thought quite differently are asked to commit to the voice of the Spirit speaking to the group as a whole. This is

---

57 Richardson and Gallagher, *Communal Wisdom*.

an essential ground rule in the Quaker approach to communal decision making,[58] discussed above.

An excellent example is found in the experience of the early Church. When Peter invited the 'believers' to choose someone to replace Judas as an apostle, his 'ground rules' were that it needed to be someone who had 'accompanied us throughout the time that the Lord Jesus went in and out among us,' they were to pray with openness to God's desire for them, and they would decide by casting lots:

> Then they prayed and said 'Lord, you know everyone's heart. Show us which one of these two you have chosen to take the place in this ministry and apostleship from which Judas turned aside to go to his own place'. And they cast lots for them, and the lot fell on Matthias. (Acts 1:24-26)

Scriptural commentators note that 'casting lots', always in a spirit of prayer and openness to God, was the traditional way in which major decisions were made. 'The lot is cast into the lap, but the decision is the Lord's alone.' (Proverbs 16:33) This expression for a way of coming to a decision may simply be another way of saying that 'a vote was taken after a period of prayerful discernment.'[59] Vacek adds that 'if God's ways are inscrutable, casting lots seems as good a way to decide as any other.'[60] In fact, he notes, that it has the advantage of eliminating bias or selfishness.

58   Lon Fendall, Jan Wood, and Bruce Bishop, *Practising Discernment Together*, 64, 114.

59   Michael Fallon, *The Acts of the Apostles* (Kensington, NSW: Chevalier Press, 2003), 40.

60   Edward C. Vacek, "Discernment within Mutual Love Relationship with God," *Theological Studies* 74, no.3 (2013): 690.

Building a Discerning Community: the common base

For communal or group discernment, the question of the group's identity is vital. A group, as a whole, will hear the promptings of God's Spirit and the attractions of spirits not-of-God only when individuals in the group have truly come together *as a group,* aware of who they are as a group. I call this their 'common base'.

Even people who have been part of a group for years seem to need time to recognise and articulate what they have always known deep-down to be their group identity. Many groups have never taken time to name who they are, how they came together and stay together, what defines their communal base, or what are their communally held values.[61] A key question for many groups is 'What precisely do we have in common?' 'What can we all commit to?' Initial, tentative answers to these questions then need to be tested, ideally by listening in prayer and sharing more deeply. Some groups begin with a motto or a Scripture text that is thought to capture their charism or define the group in some way.

The suggestions for a group's prayer around the workings of God's Spirit and other spirits *in the group* have been found to sharpen group identity, at the same time as building a discerning community.

When all members of a group spend contemplative prayer time with their agreed motto or text or common cause, the process we favour is to encourage all to share the fruits of their prayer with one another, to listen respectfully to one another and to allow others' prayer to touch their own – and then to go to prayer again. Clearly, once all in the group have heard others speak of their prayer, they will pray from a different place in themselves – with deeper awareness now of belonging to the group – when they return to prayer.

---

61   See, for example, Brian O'Leary, "Communal Discernment: An Ignatian Perspective," *Religious Life Review* 43, no. 1 (2004): 20-24. O'Leary's term is 'corporate identity'.

This process of praying, listening, praying again may need to be repeated several times. Gradually, people seem to pray more with awareness of themselves as one of the group, even while they pray individually and personally. Even when large groups are divided into smaller groups for the sake of the sharing, we've found that, provided the small groups are formed at random, listening to maybe 8-10 others *is* to be listening to the whole group. The random composition of the small group makes it representative of the whole.

When groups pray together in this way, inevitably individual members of the group are challenged around their vested interests, their blind spots and their long-held attitudes to others in the group. When individuals can honestly admit how they have been stubborn or closed to another in the group, it is not only freeing and healing for the individual, but powerfully constructive for the group. And so gradually the prayer builds a truer group identity. Examples of this process are given below when discussing the *Communal Wisdom* approach to group discernment. Group identity deepens further as the processes of communal discernment continue.

As with individual discernment, the emphasis is on a *contemplative* prayer. It seems important that people approach the prayer time genuinely wanting to hear God's Word to themselves and to the group. The same contemplative listening to others – to all others – when sharing the fruits of their prayer then follows. Neither the prayer time nor the group sharing is time for argument or debate. A pre-requisite in any process of discernment, individual or communal, is a willingness to relate honestly and openly. Only then will the members of the group hear God's Word speaking to them, individually in their quiet time and through one another in their sharing in the group. At that point, the whole process becomes an exercise of contemplative prayer.

Here is an example of communal discernment following these processes:[62]

> *The **Vita Community** is a small group of committed unmarried women, who have formally promised to live and to work for peace and reconciliation. They meet weekly for prayer and community involvement. The group has shrunk to six in number, two of whom are infirm. Somewhat to their surprise, a young woman has asked to join. The community asked me to help them to discern whether or not to accept this woman when their group seemed to be dying out.*
>
> *I offered a process of personal prayer followed by sharing of their prayer experience. My listening with them to the group's prayer would enable me to suggest a focus for ongoing prayer and sharing as the context in which to look at the decision the group wanted to make. And so we began with a prayer time focusing on the vision statement of their community: their way of life was said to witness God's merciful love, for the sake of peace in the world.*
>
> *As individuals shared the fruit of their prayer in the group, listened to others' sharing, and then prayed again (several times), there were some significant developments in the group:*
>
> - *Someone commented that their foundress, Veronica, had said that they would always be a small group, always unnoticed: it was 'better to be poorly thought-of than highly praised.' Others picked this up,*

---

62 This example is constructed from my experience of facilitating groups in processes of discernment. The *Vita* community is fictitious: some will identify with the experience, but not with the community itself.

suggesting that, as a group, they usually did think poorly of themselves: maybe what had been meant to be virtuous had become a liability? The group readily agreed to take this awareness to their next prayer time together.

- *Another woman publicly apologised to the present leader of the group for thinking negatively of her, even criticising her behind her back. In tears, the two women embraced in front of the whole group.*

- *In another sharing, an older woman shared that her prayer had given her new energy around the gift of this community and their mission – others identified with this, one person calling it their 'raison d'être'.*

It was actually well into the afternoon of their second day together that, as facilitator, I reminded the group of their initial question about the young lady who wanted to join them. Even before the group went to prayer, they knew that they had recovered their vision, they had recognised their vulnerability, and were alive. Yes, they were ready to invite others to share their life and mission.

This community of women was strongly committed to prayer. I could sense the prayerful energy in the room in the quiet times and I warmed to the honesty of their sharing and interaction. The Spirit moving in the personal prayer continued to inspire in the times of group sharing: it was as though they were still praying. The group grew *as a community,* the prayer shifting from *my* relationship with God to *our* relationship with God. The group then listens to God's Word to them, as a community.

The gifted break-throughs that happened in the *Vita* community's sharing helped the group gradually to build a community ready for discernment, open to the Spirit of God. Some spirit not-of-God could well have distracted the group at the point of their habitual 'thinking poorly of themselves', but the group seemed to recognise quickly how spirits not-of-God had tempted them at that point of vulnerability in the past, and could still. Recognising that tendency enabled the group to turn rather to the invitation of God's Spirit.

The energetic responses of different individuals to the sharing of others in the group were clear indication of God's Spirit at work. Indeed, the energy of the movements of the spirits in the group was so clear that the 'question to be discerned' was answered even before it was asked. This is a classic instance of communal discernment.

A willingness to talk openly of one's personal experience of God's Spirit in prayer and to listen contemplatively to the Spirit in the other members of the group is basic to the gradual development of 'group-think' or 'group-listening' to the Spirit. This is grace at work.[63] The *Communal Wisdom* approach recognises the Spirit of God speaking in both one's personal prayer and in one's listening: the Spirit speaks through one another in the group. Group identity builds on 'a climate of truthfulness, sincerity and mutual acceptance. The understanding, compassion and respect we exercise towards each other are mutually purifying and prepare us to discern in the voices of our brothers [and sisters] the accent of the Spirit.'[64] As a help to developing such group identity, Liebert suggests a communal practice of the Awareness Examen prayer normally reserved for individual discernment.[65]

Facilitators often encounter one or other of the predictable psychological dynamics that develop in groups: for example,

---

63 Liebert, *The Soul of Discernment*, 41.

64 Edward Malatesta, "Introduction to Discernment of Spirits," in *Discernment of Spirits* (Collegeville, MN: The Liturgical Press, 1970), 10.

65 Liebert, *The Soul of Discernment*, chapter 2. My simplified version of this prayer was mentioned earlier.

scapegoating, pairing, resistance are all common.   Group development enjoys significant breakthroughs when someone can admit to their fear or their frustration with the group process, maybe to their reaction to another person's sharing in the group, or to their concern that the group is avoiding some issue. At times, facilitators meet even communal resistance to some topic or some past experience of the group, effectively closing the group to the invitation of God's Spirit, unless faced honestly. Understanding the ways of spirits not-of-God, described in chapter 2, helps facilitators to expose such dynamics in a group.

This way of prayer and listening to one another not only builds community but has the added bonus of building the group's freedom for discernment.   In using the *Communal Wisdom* approach with groups, we have often witnessed the growth of a group as individual members are challenged around their vested interests, as happened, for example, in working with the *Vita* community. When this happens, it is often the breakthrough in the development of a group preparing for communal discernment.

Barry has used similar processes and gives examples of numerous break-throughs towards reconciliation that groups have experienced in their prayer and sharing.[66] A group's freedom for discernment flows from such growth in personal and communal new awareness.

Larkin says much the same to his brothers in chapter, prior to electing a new leadership:

> We may taste the bitterness of our hostility, for example, when we recognise that we are cultivating an 'elephant memory' that will not forgive and forget some early stupidity in an otherwise worthy candidate; or we can experience our resentment in

---

66   William A. Barry, "Towards Communal Discernment," *The Way Supplement* 58, no. Spring (1987): 110-1. William A. Barry, "Communal Discernment as a Way to Reconciliation," *Human Development* 29 (2008): 10-4.

the prejudice... against certain nationalities, races, or age groups. We can observe our blind spots, our dark side, our self-deceptions, our misplaced anger... This will help us to be more free in decision making...[67]

The *Communal Wisdom* approach has been verified in experience by its fruits: reconciliation of divisions and differences within a group, deepening relationships within a group, good decision making and new energy for mission.

Communal Vulnerability

In communal discernment, the group's vulnerability is critical. The experience of *unfreedom*, discussed earlier citing Luigi Rulla's terminology of 'essential freedom' and 'effective freedom', is shared by both individuals and groups. Rulla speaks of 'group bias':

> Every family, every religious community, and every academic or professional group must struggle daily in order to overcome the inner disintegration which threatens its functioning... or even its existence as a force for Christian vocation growth.[68]

Individual bias is well known. It is this bias that exposes a person to the false messages of spirits not-of-God. Group bias runs parallel: in exactly the same dynamic as in personal discernment, groups also have places of *unfreedom* and vulnerability. As described above, individuals experience the tempting of spirits not-of-God most frequently via false messages that they give themselves, messages that sound credible because they appeal to the person's vulnerable spot.

---

67 Ernest E. Larkin, "Guidelines for Discernment," *Human Development* 5, no. 2 (1984): 42-5.

68 Luigi M. Rulla, *Anthropology of the Christian Vocation* (Rome: Gregorian University Press,1986), 14.

A group, too, listens to false messages *as a group*, as the *Vita* community noticed when reflecting on their past experience.

Few groups seem aware of this bias in themselves and the risk of their listening to false messages. Indeed, few commentators on communal discernment seem aware of a group's vulnerability to false thinking. On the other hand, Pope John Paul's comment that the community of the People of God follows Christ 'very consciously and consistently, but at times not very consciously and very inconsistently' seems well aware of this group vulnerability.[69]

Our *Communal Wisdom* approach to group discernment sees a group's point of vulnerability critical to understanding the ways of the spirits. Several examples were given above in my discussion of the ways of spirits not-of-God.

Groups discover and name their group vulnerability by looking at the group's history of living in a discerning way and making group decisions.

---

69   John Paul II, *Redemptor Hominis* (Homebush, NSW: St. Pauls Publicaions, 1979), #86.

Chapter 5

Communal Decision Making

For the most part, groups embark on a process of communal discernment precisely because they are faced with some decision they need to make. Some groups find it very difficult to accept the facilitators' encouragement to focus on God's revealing, rather than on the decision they say they need to work on. We try to help groups to avoid thinking about and working on a possible decision: not only is there a right time to introduce the question of the decision to-be-made, but in some sense the decision will be made for us, as we keep our focus on God's revealing, as happened in the example of the *Vita* community.

Ways of making decisions

Commonly, we meet groups who ponder, discuss, research and argue the relative merits of the alternative options they face in their decision to-be-made. With this approach, invariably groups seem to remember endlessly another advantage and/or disadvantage of one or other of the options, and rarely come to a convincing decision that all can commit to.

It's true that we must research the question – a basic pre-requisite for any good discernment is to have all necessary data; and it's true that occasionally one of the options simply stands out – in which case, discernment is hardly needed. But a cognitive approach will be helpful only if and when the group is utterly free of any emotional reactions (in individuals and in the group as a whole) to the possible options. This seems to be quite rare.

In Ignatius of Loyola's celebrated teaching on the three 'times' or ways of making good decisions, he names cognitive reasoning about the perceived advantages and disadvantages of the options available as his 'third time'. Ignatius says this can be used 'in a time of tranquillity when the soul is not agitated by different spirits', and only if the decision was not able to be made in the first or second ways.[70] He seems to be saying that this cognitive way is useful as a last resort. As facilitators, we have found that such an approach can be helpful to familiarise people with the question at hand, but is rarely the way a group comes to its decision.

And so we need to look at Ignatius' first and second ways. The first is quite rare: this is when God's revelation is unmistakable, when the decision to-be-made is glaringly obvious.[71] This is not strictly discernment, since the decision is quite clear. Would that it were not so rare!

The second way involves our experience of 'desolations and consolations and the discernment of diverse spirits'.[72] This is the way of making decisions that Ignatius used most often in his own experience. He presumes that individuals and groups will most often make their decisions before God in this way. All the preliminary work with a group that we've described above is based on this presumption: that most of our decisions will flow out of some process of sifting the diverse spirits operating in the group when prayerfully considering the alternatives the group is facing.

I note that Ignatius places his teaching on decision making after a succession of meditations that he recommends to ensure that one comes to the decision making exercise quite freely.[73] Ignatius uses the term 'indifference', which he uses also in his 'First Principle and Foundation'.[74] As described earlier, citing Francis de Sales, 'indifference' is understood as freedom from

70 Ignatius Loyola, *Spiritual Exercises*, ##177-83.

71 *Ibid.*, #175.

72 *Ibid.*, #176.

73 These are the meditations on 'Two Standards' (*Spiritual Exercises*, ##136-148), 'Three Classes of Men' (##149-157), and 'Three Kinds of Humility' (##165-168)

74 Ignatius Loyola, *The Spiritual Exercises of St. Ignatius*, #23.

inner attachments, not the everyday understanding of not caring or having no reaction. This inner freedom is basic to the way of making decisions that follows.

In summary, discernment of God's will normally involve decision making in one or other of three inter-related ways:

First way	**A time when God's gift cannot be doubted**	**The decision 'makes itself'**
Second way	A time when one finds • affective movements in oneself • in relation to the alternatives	Decision is made by noting • the inner movements in oneself, • the consolations and desolations, • when contemplating the alternatives
Third way	A time of 'tranquillity' • when there are no emotional • reactions to the alternatives	Decision is made rationally, • listing pros and cons of the alternatives • and weighing against one another

Sifting the spirits

As discussed earlier, the contemplative approach to building a discerning community helps members of the group to be more aware of the movements of the spirits in their functioning as a group. In the process of preparing for discernment in this way, members of the group notice and agree on the signs when God's Spirit is active in their group and the ways their group has been – and can be – tempted at the group's vulnerable spot. As well, when God's Spirit is active in the group, members notice that relationships amongst themselves become more open and honest, and that the group grows in inner freedom. Again, this parallels the processes used in individual discernment. Here is an example of individual discernment and decision making: it offers a model for communal discernment.

> *Will, a young committed scientist, unmarried, was head-hunted and offered a new position in marine biology research, the area of his interest and expertise. The position was in a branch of CSIRO, fully government funded, recently established in Antarctica. Will sat with the offer for a couple of days and decided that he would accept – even before he had talked with anyone else about this offer of a new job. Will said, 'it just felt right'.*

> *Questions came when Will did begin to tell people. Will's parents reacted quickly. They reckoned he was crazy: why move to a place called Wilberforce ('never heard of it!') in that freezing climate. 'It couldn't possibly be good for your health.' Will's present boss could not understand why Will would accept such a pay cut. And Will's cricket mates felt let down: Will is easily their best batsman and he must know the struggle the team is having even to stay in the competition.*

> *Will came to talk with me, recommended by a mutual friend. He began by saying that he thought he had made a good decision till 'all these objections came up.'*

Will's dilemma is about how best one makes such an important decision in life, indeed how does one balance one's own preference with others' reactions.

One way of decision making, often encouraged, is to compare the advantages and disadvantages of the options that one faces (the Ignatian first way, above). Will could do that easily. This new job offer seems to have more disadvantages than advantages. Indeed, staying in his present position appears to have the advantages – no disruption, a steady salary and certain future, a good social life and good friends. If Will were to follow this method of making his decision, he may well decide to reject the offer of the new position.

The second way of making decisions is more affective than rational. This way works on the level of inner reactions. Will says that 'it just felt right', a phrase frequently heard. Hearing that and sensing the significance of it, I opted to talk with Will about this alternative way of decision making – the way, in fact, that he had used. Our conversation continued:

> *'Will, what are you actually feeling when you say that your decision felt right?' Will struggled to name his feeling. Words came slowly: 'it felt right... like good and true... maybe I felt at home with the possibility, at ease, comfortable... even contented. It's hard to put words on feelings, isn't it?' 'OK, I said 'so what you are saying is that feeling comfortable and content with the thought of the new job seemed right to you. I wonder what makes it right? Is it a familiar feeling for you? You must have felt this before?' Will said 'I don't think I have put words on it quite like I have now, but yes, I do know this feeling. Even in little decisions every day, whenever I feel like this, I know I'm in the right place.' I could see that Will was actually trusting his own past experience, fairly spontaneously recognising that this inner experience, however difficult to articulate, was actually a sign for him of the right way to go. Because it had paid off in the past. This seemed more important to Will (and to me) than all the arguments for and against such a decision.*

I asked Will about the different reactions of his friends. He reckoned that he could understand what they were saying and he would certainly want to be sensitive in his helping them to accept his decision. But 'I believe that if this is best for me, it will end up being good for others, too.' 'OK, so where are you now?' I asked. Will said quickly 'Oh, I'm going. I'm excited about the new possibilities. I'm looking forward to contributing to some worthwhile research.'

In Will's experience, the two ways of making his decision, the more rational and the more affective, would appear to result in different outcomes. Will has learned from past experience to 'trust his gut', even though he finds it difficult to explain. In fact, this way of making a decision that Will followed is quite common. It is very personal. The signs of what is right for Will are unique to Will. Others will say 'it's not rational'!

So, too, with groups learning to trust their past experience of the spirits. Facilitators sense when the group is ready – relating openly and freely, and in touch with the movements of the spirits – to hear the options they face in the decision to-be-made. The plan is to look at the options in the decision to-be-made, one at a time, alongside the known indicators of when and how the group is following God's invitation and when and how the group can be tempted away from God.

Rahner, writing in the persona of Ignatius Loyola, expresses the process in this way:

> When I placed the available possibilities and their potential outcomes before me in light of the impending free choice to be made, I discovered that one option clearly fitted into the wide freedom of God and remained transparent toward him, while the other did not, even though all options could be small signs of this infinite God which,

each in its own way, derived from him. While it is difficult to make clear, this is approximately how I learned to distinguish... between what held the incomprehensibility of the infinite God who wanted to be near me and what remained somewhat dark and non-transparent toward God...[75]

One remains 'transparent toward God' via the discernment of one's 'experience of consolations and desolations', in Ignatius' earlier terminology.

Essential to this step in the process is that the group looks contemplatively at each option separately, one at a time. The facilitators encourage group members to take option A to prayer and to listen to God's word as they have been doing in building their community, *as though A is the decision already made.* Each member of the group, and later the group as a whole during the sharing time, will begin to notice how they are moved in their prayer with option A. As before, the prayer time may need to be repeated after hearing others share the fruits of their prayer, until the point is reached where the whole group senses how they, as a group, are affected by option A. People may recognise quite quickly the significance of this inner movement in their group, because of their earlier sharing around the signs of the spirits. It may be obvious to them that A is God's call – in which case, they may make their decision without even having to pray with option B. On the other hand, the facilitators may judge that the group would benefit from the same process of prayer and sharing with option B. This could be as a way of confirming that option A is the best group decision before God, or it could be because option A does not seem to sit well with the group's past experience of the working of God's Spirit. And so, once again, the group's noticing the inner movements in themselves as they pray with this second option, and in the

---

75 Karl Rahner, *Ignatius of Loyola Speaks*, trans. Annemarie S. Kidder (South Bend, IN: St. Augustine's Press, 2013), 19.

group during their sharing, will tell them something of God's call in relation to option B.

Usually there comes a time in prayer and group sharing when it is quite clear that one or other option is consistent with the way the group already knows God works in them: they recognise the signs. Then the group's decision is made quite easily, confident that their decision will be life-giving for themselves and for others. This was the experience of the *Vita* community.

Again, this is not to say that the group necessarily reaches consensus. Not every member of the group will necessarily agree with this decision personally; but every member does agree willingly and happily to abide by what is clearly the group decision. Once again, the group is bigger than, different from, the sum of the parts.

Confirmation of the group's decision comes gradually, as the decision is lived out in people's everyday lives. Often, only afterwards, people begin to recognise benefits of their decision that they hadn't anticipated. They may notice, for example, how the group is more harmonious or how members of the group are more content in their ministry to others. Such fruits of the decision are the real confirmation.

Conclusion

Communal discernment parallels personal discernment. Communal decision making, like personal decision making, rests on the group's prior work on their group identity, their communal relationship with God and their awareness of the ways of the spirits in their group experience. Though a somewhat foreign concept for many groups, group experience of the spirits is quite a different reality from the sum of the experiences of all the members of the group.

Time spent in developing group identity and awareness is time well spent. The Appendix details some practical helps towards such development, particularly the various ways of contemplative prayer together.

In relation to communal decision making, the group's inner freedom is pre-requisite. As in individual discernment and decision making, awareness of the group's vulnerability to the tempting of spirits not-of-God and recognition of the false messages appealing to the point of vulnerability frees the group to reject the falsity and respond to God's invitation.

The Church's emphasis on collaborative leadership and involvement of laity in Church structures invites new opportunity for considerable development in communal discernment. The principles and practice of communal discernment that I have outlined could well assist parish pastoral teams and diocesan synods, chapters of religious congregations, even Bishops' conferences and plenary councils.

Appendix

Helps to Communal Discernment

How *a group* relates to God is a rather foreign concept for many groups. And so, how a group might *discern* God's call – as distinct from 'discuss, debate or argue' – can be equally foreign. Hence our emphasis on building a discerning community and establishing a group identity. We emphasise that this group awareness is not merely the sum of all the individual members' ways of being and praying and relating to God. Though the group is composed of individuals who all contribute, *the group* experience is a whole different reality.

Some commentators have suggested that, whereas Western spiritualities tend to emphasise our individuality and our personal uniqueness, Eastern spiritualities focus more on our sameness and our oneness. Certainly, Eastern spiritualities recognise better that uniqueness and oneness are not exclusive of one another. Some of the practices of the East can be quite helpful in the development of a communal consciousness.

Many know the experience of the bonds that can develop in a group of people who sit together for an extended time, with a common purpose, but in total silence, as in Quaker practice. Or the group awareness that builds amongst people who are together on retreat, even without any conversation to one another.

Some of the ways of prayer that we've learned from the East can have the same effect. For example, in the so-called 'prayer of the breath'[76], I might sit alone focusing on my own breathing, gradually deepening and slowing down the inhalations and exhalations. At a point where the rhythm of the breathing has stilled the body and mind, I may begin with some words

---

76   Abhishiktananda, *Prayer* (London: SPCK, 1967).

like 'Breathe in me, Breath of God', recited repetitively to the same rhythm. In itself, this is a powerful gesture of prayer, surrendering to the God who breathes in me. But, over and above that – and this is the point for our present purposes – what often happens is that I seem to be drawn beyond awareness of my own breathing, even of God's breathing in me, to some sense of God's breathing in all people, in all creation. I become aware, rather, of our oneness, our unity before God. Groups wishing to build a discerning community would benefit greatly from such prayer together.

Another example is the Buddhist/Christian practice of 'mindfulness'.[77] Mindfulness is to be fully present to what I'm doing when I'm doing it. The Christian parallel is the teaching on *The Sacrament of the Present Moment*[78], believing that every activity in every moment has the potential to be a meeting place with God. It may seem quite remote from a need for discernment to be giving one's full attentiveness to washing the dishes or admiring the autumn leaves as I stroll down a laneway, or listening to another person's story as the other shares with me. My experience is that the unexpected gift of such a habit of mindfulness is that I am often lifted beyond the focus of my attention: while I'm totally present to and absorbed in the beauty of the laneway or the person I'm in conversation with, I find myself aware of my oneness with the other and our oneness in God. Again, such a practice could be ideal preparation for members of a group wishing to discern God's call together.

The longing for oneness with others, breaking the barriers that separate people, is a universal human experience. In some sense, the very longing is already to know the oneness.[79] Maybe the best starting point for any group embarking on

---

77   Thich Nhat Hanh, *The Miracle of Mindfulness* (London: Random House, 1991).

78   Jean-Paul de Caussade SJ, *Self-Abandonment to Divine Providence* (Glasgow: Collins, Fontana, 1972) and *The Sacrament of the Present Moment* (London: Collins, 1981).

79   Brian Gallagher MSC, *Taking God to Heart: A Living Spirituality* (Strathfield NSW: St Pauls Publications, 2008), 17-18.

group discernment is their desire to hear God's word to them as a group. Often in the process of building the discerning community and discerning the questions before the group, the facilitators will bring the group back to their deepest desire.

Recommended Reading

Aschenbrenner, George. "Consciousness Examen." *Review for Religious* 31, no. 1 (1972): 14-21.

Fendall, Lon, Wood, Jan and Bishop. Bruce. *Practising Discernment Together: Finding God's Way Forward in Decision Making*. Newberg, OR: Barclay Press, 2007.

Futrell, John Carroll. "Ignatian Discernment." *Studies in the Spirituality of Jesuits* II, no. 2 (1970).

Futrell, John Carroll. "Communal Discernment." *Studies in the Spirituality of Jesuits* IV, no. 5 (1972).

Gallagher, Brian. *Pray as You Are*. Sydney, NSW: Nelen Yubu, 1999.

Gallagher, Brian. *Taking God to Heart*. Strathfield, NSW: St Pauls, 2008.

Ignatius Loyola. *The Spiritual Exercises of St Ignatius Loyola*. Edited by George E. Gans. Chicago, IL: Loyola University Press, 1998.

Liebert, Elizabeth. *The Soul of Discernment*. Louisville, Ky: Westminster John Knox Press, 2015.

Lonsdale, David. *Dance to the Music of the Spirit*. London: Darton, Longman & Todd, 1992.

McKinney, Mary Benet. *Sharing Wisdom: A Process for Group Decision Making*. Allen, Texas: Tabor Publishing, 1987.

Rahner, Karl. *Ignatius of Loyola Speaks*. Translated by Annemarie S. Kidder. South Bend, IN: St. Augustine's Press, 2013.

Rulla, Luigi M. "The Discernment of Spirits and Christian Anthropology." *Gregorianum* 59, no. 3 (1978): 537-69.